D1501012

Salesian

Pearls of Wisdom

*A little guidebook to
authentic holiness*

with

St. Francis de Sales
as our guide

compiled by
Sr. John Marie Schauber OSFS

DEDICATION

This little guidebook is dedicated to all of the Oblate Fathers, Brothers, and Sisters of St. Francis de Sales, who strive each day to live out these pearls of wisdom.

May their gentle, humble witness to Salesian spirituality draw many others to join them on St. Francis de Sales' path to holiness.

Foreword
By Rev. Alexander Pocetto, OSFS

The proliferation of books, pamphlets, and websites, etc., on the spirituality of St. Francis de Sales is truly astonishing and gives eloquent testimony to its durability and effectiveness of speaking to the human heart. Because Salesian spirituality has its roots deeply implanted in the Holy Spirit, whom the saint calls "Holy Love," it readily accommodates our individual strengths and circumstances in creative and surprising ways. In a very real sense, it is a customized spirituality whose contours follow the shape and the needs of one's state in life. This is its real genius.

Sr. John Marie has a solid and experiential understanding of this genius and has captured it in a very appealing and disarming manner. The saint believed that "wisdom is knowledge whereby one savors, tests and penetrates the goodness of the law and the revealed things of the gospels, not in order to speak or preach about them, but to practice them" (OEA, IX, p. 33). In presenting these "Salesian Pearls of Wisdom," she captures the heart of the saint's wisdom and makes it readily accessible to all.

The image of a journey emphasized in this work stresses its progressive and intentional aspects, one that urges us to continually move forward despite whatever setbacks we may experience. Wisely, the author allows for reflections after each pearl so that we can catch our breath and move at our own pace, or more precisely, at the pace we understand God wants us to advance.

This work exudes the saint's optimistic and encouraging spirit, one that builds on our strengths and bolsters our weaknesses. As we dwell and reflect on the various pearls, we gain greater insight into who we are and who God wants us to become. So it is a journey that is intended to take us to the depths of our heart, to the depths of our being.

This might at first appear to be a daunting task, but Sr. John Marie reassures us that she accompanies us and supports us with her prayers and with the saint's "inspired commonsense," as Elisabeth Stopp, a very renowned Salesian writer, so aptly described it.

♣ *Introduction* ♣

Why another book on St. Francis De Sales? Is there not an abundance of books on his life, spirituality, writings, letters, homilies, and teachings? There is indeed a wonderful abundance.

However, allow me to explain the events that brought into existence this little book that you are now holding. The idea to publish a book on Salesian spirituality came in little nudges that kept popping up persistently in the most unexpected circumstances.

The first nudge came when I was teaching juniors at DeSales University in Center Valley, Pennsylvania. The class was composed of student teachers who had entered quite seriously into their academic journey, and as I began my first class, I suggested that we start with a Direction of Intention. The students looked at me quite quizzically and several asked, "What is a Direction of Intention?"

It saddened me to realize that these young people who were now in their third year at DeSales University were clueless about this spiritual nugget given to us by St. Francis.

The second nudge came when I was giving spiritual direction to two staff members. Both had been working at DeSales for a number of years. Several weeks into their individual sessions, I referred to the Direction of Intention. Again, I was sadly surprised to learn that neither one had ever heard of it.

However, it was thrilling to see how easily they absorbed this spiritual activity and began to use it on a daily basis and to experience first-hand its great benefit.

The third nudge came as I was preparing and giving an online course, "Salesian Pearls of

Wisdom," during Lent. Because it was a brief five-week course, I wanted to cover the most important, practical, salient, and attractive of the various "pearls" that make up Salesian spirituality. I chose the Direction of Intention as one of the weekly "pearls" and gave a little explanation and some background on this wonderful Salesian activity.

The students in the online class responded enthusiastically with these various encouraging comments:

*"This was for me a **WOW** moment!"*

"The Direction of Intention is making such a difference in my life. I am so much more peaceful now. Things still go wrong, but I don't lose my peace."

"Learning about the spiritual pearls of wisdom was like being reunited with an old friend. For example, I had heard 'Bloom where you are planted.' all my life but never connected it to the spiritual path."

And, finally, the most affirming for me:

"Learning about Salesian pearls of wisdom has made this the best Lent I have ever spent!"

These nudges made it very clear that, indeed, another book is needed, a simple book much like a treasured guidebook, pages well-worn from use, that you might carry with you as you hike through mountain paths, an unpretentious book that would lay out the beauty and practicality of Salesian spirituality for all who seek to deepen their spiritual life. I hope that this will be for you a little guidebook that will gently reveal the Salesian pearls of wisdom which, if nurtured and cultivated carefully, become real stepping stones to authentic holiness.

♣ *Who is St. Francis de Sales?* ♣

For anyone who might not be familiar with St. Francis de Sales, here is a short biography:

Francis was born in 1567, in the Duchy of Savoy in the region that is now a part of France. The oldest among his siblings, he was expected to carry out his father's plans to be a lawyer. He was sent to the finest schools of the time and eventually earned a doctorate in both civil and canon law.

His real dream, however, was to become a priest. With the help of some influential friends, he finally obtained permission to pursue this vocation. Francis lived a holy priesthood and was eventually made a bishop. With St. Jane de Chantal in 1610, he founded a religious order, the Visitation of Holy Mary.

St. Francis was a noted preacher, writer and spiritual director. He counseled hundreds of people from every walk of life, especially through written correspondence. Those letters formed the foundation for his book *Introduction to the Devout Life*.

St. Francis developed a gentle spirituality of the heart, focused on humility, gentleness, and goodness toward one's neighbor. It has been named Salesian after his family name of Sales. One of his most famous maxims sums up his spirituality beautifully*:*

> ***"All through love,
> nothing through force."***

♣ *A Message* ♣

My dear friend,

My name is Sr. John Marie and I am an Oblate Sister of St. Francis de Sales. Please do not find me too forward in addressing you as friend. It is possible that I do not know you and may not have the pleasure of meeting you; however, the fact that you are reading this book turns our acquaintance into a spiritual friendship. I promised myself that if this little book ever made it to publication, then from that day forward I would pray daily and ask God's blessing on those who would choose to read it to discover or rediscover the treasures of Salesian spirituality.

The book follows a simple format. I have chosen nine Salesian pearls of wisdom. Each one is explained and some background is given.

Following that, a few reflections and challenges are offered.

This book is written with two different groups of people in mind. First, it is for those who just want to learn more about Salesian spirituality. People who have met the Oblate Fathers, Brothers, and Sisters for the first time, for example, are often curious when they see how much the Oblates are loved and appreciated by those who work with them. They begin to wonder: what is it that sets them apart from others? What exactly is this Salesian spirituality that they live?

If you are in this first group, you may want to skip the reflections and just concentrate on the narrative about each pearl and what Francis has to say about it. I hope you will find it helpful.

Second, it is for those who are looking for a deeper spiritual life, who are seeking a more authentic prayer life, who are spiritually hungry for a holiness of life. This little guidebook will provide the way.

If you are in the second group and you make the time and effort to absorb the wisdom behind each pearl, if you commit to practicing and living out the spiritual activity attached to each of the nine pearls and you gently cultivate them in your spiritual life, I can promise that you will be well on your way to holiness.

I will be walking this journey with you because I also yearn to deepen my understanding and my commitment to these simple but deeply profound spiritual activities. So let us journey together, supporting each other in prayer and spiritual friendship. I am excited to be on this path with you! With your little guidebook in hand, let us begin our walk

♣ Salesian Pearls of Wisdom ♣

1. *Be who you are, and be that well.*

2. *Bloom where you are planted.*

3. *Live in the present moment.*

4. *Make the Direction of Intention.*

5. *Practice little aspirations.*

6. *Be patient with yourself!*

7. *Practice the little virtues!*

8. *Be at peace!*

9. *Live + Jesus*

♣ *Pearl One* ♣

Be who you are,
*   and be that well.*

This first Salesian pearl is taken from a familiar maxim of St. Francis de Sales: "Be who you are and be that well." Let us pause for a moment and simply reflect on those words... What does it mean to **be who you are?**

Shakespeare wrote, *"To thine own self, be true."* Plato, the famous philosopher said, *"Know thyself."* Julius Hare, a chaplain to Queen Victoria, wrote: *"Be what you are. This is the first step toward becoming better than you are."* Therefore, we can be assured that these are important and deep things that we are considering.

But how do you really come to know yourself? Is it by recognizing your gifts, talents, and weaknesses and defects that you come to know yourself? Is it the work you do, or perhaps the vocation you live out that defines you? Is it all of these together? Is there more to it than this? Have you perhaps allowed someone else to define who you are?

Matthew Kelly, a modern spiritual leader and writer, speaks often about becoming the best version of ourselves. Is that what St. Francis means by "…**be that well**"?

Perhaps some background will help here. We turn, of course, to our guide St. Francis.

St. Francis actually wrote this maxim in a letter to one of his directees in 1605. (A directee is someone who has a spiritual director or spiritual companion.) This particular directee was Madame Brûlart, the wife of Nicolas Brûlart, who served as president of the Burgundian Parliament.

Madame Brûlart was energetic, and somewhat anxious. She felt that she could never attain holiness in the midst of all the splendor of the court and in the busyness of the many responsibilities of her married life.

Francis was very patient with her and gently

tried to help her see that holiness can be achieved anywhere and is meant for everyone. Here are his words to her…and to us.

"Be attentive, my dearest child, to make yourself every day more pure of heart. This purity consists in weighing all things in the balance of that sanctuary, which is nothing other than the will of God.
I refer to your desires. It seems to me that white is not the color proper to roses, for red roses are more beautiful and more fragrant; however, white is the distinctive characteristic of lilies. ***Let us be what we are and be that well****, in order to bring honor to the Master Craftsman whose handiwork we are."* (Thy Will Be Done, pp. 21-22)

Some reflections:

We are presented with our first Salesian pearl of wisdom:

- Ponder carefully what it means to know yourself.
- Spend time reflecting deeply on what it means to be the best version of yourself.
- Gently take time to discover what God desires for you.

Stay with these thoughts and reflections for as long as you need. Let us pause on our spiritual journey keeping our guidebook on hand.

When we have really discovered who we are called to be, I believe that we will have uncovered our truest selves. This authenticity should begin to guide how we speak, how we think, how we act and interact, how we perceive, how we choose, and how we treat others.

Reflectively re-read St. Francis' response to Madame Brûlart as if he had written it to you.

Spend time with this spiritual advice. You have taken your first step toward genuine holiness and the ground is fertile for our second pearl but first, my friend, a little word of warning.

Please don't think because you perhaps now have a clearer understanding of who you are and you possess the desire to be genuinely true to yourself that the battle is won. You will soon discover that holiness is the work of a lifetime. Each day we will fail and each time we must get up and start over again, continually striving anew…to be who we are. Each day we must take up our spiritual journey with fresh courage. This great and marvelous journey will only really end at the moment of our death. When you are ready, I invite you to pearl two.

♣ *Pearl Two* ♣

Bloom where you are planted.

Our first pearl, "Be who you are and be that well," leads beautifully into this next spiritual maxim from Francis.

"Bloom where you are planted."

There is a lovely elementary school in Australia named after St. Francis de Sales and the school motto is, *"Bloom where you are planted."*

Interestingly, I have found this quote in sources completely outside of Salesian spirituality. There are several gardening clubs, for example, and even spiritual gathering groups that use *"Bloom where you are planted"* as their title. As far as I can tell, they have no affiliation with Salesian spirituality. This thought also has been found in a list of ancient proverbs from Afghanistan. We can assume from this that Francis didn't actually coin the phrase as we know it today but that he definitely understood it and taught it to his directees. He lived it fully himself as well. Exiled as a bishop from his own diocese of Geneva, Switzerland, he bloomed beautifully in Annecy, France, where he even founded a religious order, the Sisters of the Visitation of Holy Mary.

One example of Francis' encouragement to live out this spiritual maxim is found in a letter he wrote to the curé (pronounced cure-ray) of Gex, a region in France. In Francis' time, a curé was a pastor.

Francis was Bishop of Geneva but was barred from his diocese because of the persecution of Catholics in Switzerland, so he lived in Annecy, France. He founded his first convent of the Visitation Sisters in Annecy, very near the famous lake of Annecy. In the northern side of the huge lake was the region of Gex, which was French territory.

This pastor of Gex evidently had met Francis and had a correspondence with him from time to time to get help and advice. We can assume that he struggled with feeling unsuccessful as a pastor and wondered if he couldn't be more productive doing something else.

We can also assume that Francis had advised him on this more than once from the context of the letter, *"I persist always in telling you…"*

Here is Francis' response to him:

*"I persist always in telling you that you ought to serve God **where you are** and **do what you are doing**. Not, my dear brother, that I would wish to hinder the growth of your good works nor the continual purification of your heart; but **do what you are doing and do it better if you can**. Take my advice and **remain where you are**; do faithfully all you honestly can do and you will experience how, if you believe, you will see the glory of God. If you wish to do well, regard as temptation all that may be suggested to you as to change of place; for, while your*

mind is elsewhere you can never give your full attention to make progress where you are." (Francis de Sales, Jane de Chantal, Letters of Spiritual Direction, p.179)

Very practical advice! ***Bloom where you are planted!*** We also have a glimpse of this perspective in another letter Francis wrote to Madame Brûlart.

Our last meeting with Madame Brûlart was in the letter quoted in the first pearl. This new letter is dated June, 1607. At this time, she had been under his direction for two years. Let us take a close look at Francis' response to Marie Brûlart. Without actually using the quote he manages to capture its essence:

"...persevere in overcoming yourself in the little everyday frustrations that bother you; let your best efforts be directed there. God wishes nothing else of you at present, so don't waste

*time doing anything else. **Don't sow your desires in someone else's garden; just cultivate your own as best you can; don't long to be other than what you are, but desire to be thoroughly what you are. Believe me that this is the most important and the least understood point in the spiritual life. What is the use of building castles in Spain when we have to live in France?"*** (Francis de Sales, Jane de Chantal, Letters of Spiritual Direction, p.112)

Francis definitely lived and taught the proverb:

"Bloom where you are planted."

Some reflections:

Are we sure we know who is doing the planting in **"Bloom where you are planted"**? Did God place me here as a part of God's plan for me...or is it possible that I got myself here by my own choices?

For example, if, at this point in my life, I have completely abandoned any practice of the faith tradition handed on to me by my parents, did God plant me in this environment or did a series of my own choices put me here, totally contrary to what God's plan might have been?

If I have goals of having an extremely lucrative career, is God doing the planting or am I as I work hard to achieve my goal of great wealth?

For us as Christians, does not everything ultimately depend on what God's will is for each of us? If I perceive that where I am is clearly God's will for me, then God is doing the planting. If I know in my heart that where I am is in contradiction to God's will, do I not have to move to another place (not necessarily a geographical place, but rather a change in my outlook and attitude) and begin to bloom from this new place?

My friend, I encourage you to spend quiet time with these little reflections. They are the very foundation of your spiritual journey and to your longing for holiness. This pearl, in particular, holds the reward of true peace of heart.

My caution for this pearl: Be careful not to assume that you must <u>feel</u> happy in order to bloom where you are. It is relatively easy to "bloom" when everything is going well. The real question is: can we steadfastly bloom when we are in a place of sadness? A loved one has passed away, a friend has betrayed us, or we have lost our job. Do we have enough trust and peace of heart to stay the course and gently put forth blooms even in our darkness?

Stay with this pearl and these reflections for as long as you need. There is no need to hurry on the spiritual journey. You have already come a long way if you are striving to live each day to:

"Be who you are and be that well."

You have also come far if, in whatever place you find yourself at this time in your life, you are learning to **"Bloom where you are planted"** in accordance with God's plans for you.

Again, read Francis' words as if they were written directly to you. Absorb them into your heart and strive to live them out each day.

I find it very helpful to give shortened names to the things I am working on in my spiritual journey. I can then repeat them as mantras during the day. The word *mantra* comes from Sanskrit and refers to a thought chosen to assist us. *Mantras* are words or groups of words that are repeated with the goal of creating a positive transformation within ourselves. Many persons, for example, use the Jesus prayer as their mantra: *"Jesus, have pity on me."*

Throughout the day, from time to time, the mantra is gently repeated in the silence of our hearts, grounding us in a prayerful and focused attentiveness to God and to ourselves.

If this works for you, we can say we have studied and are practicing the living out of our first two pearls with these two simple mantras:

- **"Be authentic"** when you are tempted to put on a façade, to speak an untruth, to give in to peer pressure, gently whisper this mantra in your heart for strength and courage.

- **"Bloom here"** when you are tempted to blame others, to complain and nag, to find fault, gently whisper this mantra in your heart to gain the peace you need in order to bloom.

My dear friend, a gentle reminder:

These two Salesian pearls are the most life-changing if we allow them to be. They really are attitudes and ways of living that we choose to adopt and nurture. The other pearls on which we will reflect will tend more to spiritual activities and exercises, but these two, I believe, are different; they are really fundamental to living out Salesian spirituality.

To make room for them in our lives, however, we need to let go of all that might hinder their growth. Before we can **bloom**, we may need to **prune.**

What hinders the growth of these two pearls will be different for each of us, but generally it will be things like: holding on to grudges and judgment of others, unwillingness to forgive others or ourselves, giving in to peer pressure and failing to keep watch over our words and our thoughts, or failure to nurture our prayer life. The list could be endless.

May I suggest that we stop here in our spiritual journey and spend some time with these thoughts?

Let us do a little soul-searching to discover our response to two important questions:

- What areas in my life need some pruning in order to continue on this spiritual journey toward holiness?

- Is my yearning for a deeper and holier life still strong enough that I want to continue this journey?

These questions are crucial. Please take all the time you need to ponder them and to find your own personal authentic response to each question. No one can lead us to holiness…a spiritual friend can only accompany and companion us.

The work to be done, the struggles to see the journey through, the yearning for the journey must come from deep within us. Do not rush or force your responses…listen gently to your own heart.

Salesian spirituality is a spirituality of the heart!

After you have rested a bit, I invite you to explore pearl three.

♣ *Pearl Three* ♣

Live in the Present Moment.

One of the appealing tenets in the spirituality of St. Francis de Sales is his understanding of the value of the "present moment." When directees sought him out or wrote to him, often they carried two heavy burdens: shame and guilt for past actions or fear and dread for what the future might hold. He would attempt to bring them to understand that the present moment, the moment we are living through right now, is the only one that is ours. All else we must surrender to God's love and mercy.

We cannot change any of our actions of the past; we can, however, surrender the past to God's mercy, and then give it no further thought. If worry for the future wears us down, Francis would encourage us to surrender that also into our heavenly Father's hands and concentrate on living well the present moment.

This is wonderful advice to help keep us focused and intentional through the day.

This time, we encounter a Mademoiselle de Soulfour who was a young religious in Paris. She was still quite new to the religious life. Having very high ideals of perfection, she had difficulty in accepting human weakness in herself and in the nuns with whom she lived.

She had confided to Francis her disillusionment and uncertainties and told him of her wish to enter the more strict Carmelite order. Does that sound a little bit like a "Bloom where you are planted" problem?

Actually, it was a "Stay in the present moment" problem. Mademoiselle de Soulfour had just recovered from a period of spiritual distress because she had so many lofty desires which in the end she had not achieved. When Francis is writing to her, the spiritual crisis had passed but she was sad and nervous and worried about her spiritual future. Francis is very gentle and patient with this intense religious. Here is his response to her:

"I recommend to you holy simplicity. Look straight in front of you and not at the dangers you see in the distance. Let us be firmly resolved to serve God with our whole heart and life.

Beyond that, let us have no care for tomorrow. Let us think only of living today well, and when tomorrow comes, it will also be today and we can think about it then." (Francis de Sales,. Jane de Chantal, Letters of Spiritual Direction, pp. 98-99)

It seems to me that everything about the spirituality of St. Francis de Sales leads to balance, trust, optimism, and practicality.

I thought you might find it interesting that, in the end, she did not follow Francis's advice and she did transfer to the Carmelite Sisters where she seems to have lived happily until her death in 1633. God has unique plans for each of us!

Some reflections:

- To arrive at that state of perfect trust takes a lot of surrender and, sometimes, we are just not comfortable making that surrender because it means letting go. Letting go can be very hard. As you reflect on the words of Francis to Mademoiselle de Soulfour, see where you stand with his teaching.

- Keep in mind that when Francis says we should leave the future in God's hands, he doesn't mean we shouldn't plan for the future. We are bound to do that according to our responsibilities in life. He does mean, however, that we shouldn't fret and worry, but trust in his providence to get us through each challenge.

All of the pieces of this multifaceted pearl confirm something that I shared with you early on in our spiritual journey: this learning to trust, to surrender, to focus on the present moment will not happen in a few days of efforts. The spiritual journey is the work of a lifetime.

Remember this pearl when you are tempted to give up. Open your guidebook to this page and re-read his gentle encouragement for you to live the present moment as best as you can. Remind yourself that the present moment is all that really counts. Live this present moment well and, my dear friend, all will be well.

When you feel ready, please turn to pearl four.

♣ *Pearl Four* ♣

Make the Direction of Intention.

Let me start by telling you that this is my favorite pearl. For the Oblate Fathers, Brothers and Sisters, it is the heart of our spirituality.

It refers to the action of pausing before each new action and focusing our attention on lifting this action to God. It is elegantly simple and profoundly powerful.

In his vision for holiness for persons in all walks of life, Francis saw the Direction of Intention as a means by which the simple, everyday acts could be transformed into something holy, sacred, and sublime. The most insignificant actions could become a spiritual experience!

The historical background of the Direction of Intention stems from a rule book that Francis composed for himself while he was a student at the University of Padua. With the help of his spiritual director, Antonio Possevino, a Jesuit, he composed a series of guidelines to keep his heart focused amid the temptations and turmoil of university life. This guidebook contained the Direction of Intention.

Francis realized the power behind this simple act and later he taught it to St. Jane de Chantal. When they founded together the Congregation of the Visitation Sisters, they gave the Sisters a booklet entitled *Spiritual Directory for Daily Actions.* This booklet, which was intended to help the Sisters live an authentic spiritual life, contained a teaching on the Direction of Intention.

Two hundred years later, when Father Brisson founded the Congregations of the Oblate Sisters and of the Oblate Fathers and Brothers of St. Francis de Sales, he passed the *Spiritual Directory for Daily Actions* on to us. Here is what Francis wrote at the beginning of this little booklet.

"May your whole life, and everything you do tend to unite you with God. May your prayers, good works, and the practice of all the Christian virtues, above all that of charity, contribute to the life of the Church and to the salvation of your neighbor.

For this reason, may you desire nothing so much as to live an intensely spiritual life; then, while pleasing God, your power for good may be communicated to the hearts of the faithful."
(In the Midst of the World, p.4)

Among the spiritual guidelines of the precious booklet, there was one dedicated to the Direction of Intention. Here's what Francis wrote for this topic:

"Those who wish to thrive and to advance in the way of Our Lord should, at the beginning of each of their actions, both interior and exterior, ask for his grace and offer to his divine

goodness all the good they will do. In this way, they will be prepared to bear with peace and serenity all the pain and suffering they will encounter as coming from the fatherly hand of our good God and Savior whose most holy purpose is to have them merit by such means so as to reward them afterwards with the abundance of his love.

They should not neglect this practice in matters which are small and seemingly insignificant, nor even if they are engaged in those things which are agreeable and in complete conformity with their own will and needs such as eating, drinking, resting, recreating and similar actions; by following the advice of the Apostle, everything they do will be done in God's name, to please him alone. (Spiritual Directory of St. Francis de Sales, pp.23-24)

For me, the utter simplicity of this action and its profoundly transformative power are mindboggling.

You don't need to be in a church, you don't need any rituals; you just need to pause for an instant before starting the action, and offer it to God as gift. You can use the prayer familiar to the Oblates, "O my God, I give this action to you. Help me to conduct myself in a manner most pleasing to you." You can also just use the words that come from the center of your heart such as, "My God, this is for you. I give it with love."

Nothing is too trivial to be given as gift:

Doing the laundry

Writing a birthday card

Taking a shower

Walking the dog

...each becomes a spiritual gift, a prayer, an act of love.

Some reflections:

There are three important benefits to this Direction of Intention:

1. If there is some pain or difficulty in the action, somehow it is received with a greater serenity because we paused before the action to turn it over to God as gift and to ask for his help.

2. By the same token, if there is special pleasure in the action (enjoying a birthday party, taking an afternoon nap, relishing a good book, packing a picnic for a family outing, etc.), that pleasure itself becomes holy because you took time to lift the action to God.

3. Your prayer life is deepened because of these little connections with God woven through your day. A short prayer, a glance, is all that is needed to take the simplest action and bring it to God.

For me this Direction of Intention also calls to mind the childhood fairytale of Rumpelstiltskin that many of us enjoyed. In the story, the miller's daughter is locked in a room and told that she must turn straw into gold, or her father will die. It was her father who bragged to the king that his daughter could do anything, even turn straw into gold. The poor girl is weeping bitterly when Rumpelstiltskin comes on the scene and spins the straw into gold for her. Perhaps, you remember that all ends well in the fairytale.

The part I want to focus on is the miller's daughter weeping because she knows she cannot turn straw into gold.

For us, the wonderful news is: with the Direction of Intention, we have the awesome power to turn the straw of our everyday lives, the straw of the many mundane actions we perform each day, into the gold of love of God.

It is a tiny spiritual action that can produce monumental spiritual benefits.

On a random blog I happened to come upon, a beautiful young woman of Jewish, Buddhist background was asked by her friends how she prays. She shared her daily prayer ritual:

 "I get in the shower each morning and I repeat this mantra: *May all my thoughts, words, and actions come from a place of love.*"

On my way to class, I use this mantra: *"May every action be a prayer of Love in the world."* What a beautiful form of the Direction of Intention!

My dear friend, take time to soak in all the beautiful facets of the Direction of Intention. However, I also offer a warning. It takes time to form the habit of remembering to make the Direction of Intention before beginning an action. For some of us, it takes a very long time. One could easily give up, but I beg of you not to give in to that temptation.

Ask for the help of the Holy Spirit. Start with small, baby steps. Promise to make the Direction of Intention for three or four of those actions you do routinely each day: eating breakfast, taking a shower, checking your mail.

Practice in those areas for several days or weeks until you find yourself making a Direction of Intention naturally for each of them. Then you can move on to add a few more until one day you discover that you involve God and a desire to please him in each of your actions, that you are living the actions of each day with love and prayerfulness. This is truly a powerful activity. Take a little rest and then I invite you to continue to pearl five.

♣ *Pearl Five* ♣

Practice little aspirations.

There is another little prayer activity that comes out of Salesian spirituality. This little prayer form is referred to by many of us Oblates as "aspirations," which are short prayers that Francis would have us say as we move through the day.

For those persons who really may not have large chunks of time to pray...well, here is the answer! Carry a few of these aspirations in your heart, and from time to time throughout the day repeat them gently from your heart.

Francis starts by giving us some suggested samples to memorize:

- Yes, my Father, yes, always yes! (a good one when you are experiencing a difficulty)
- Lord, may I live for you alone.

- Queen of heaven, I entrust my soul to you.
- Jesus, be to me a Jesus. (meaning, be to me a Savior at this moment)
- My God, when will I love you perfectly?
- Holy Guardian Angel, watch over me. (a good one when traveling)

Francis' hope, however, was that once this had become a habit, then you would no longer need memorized prayers.

- You begin to personalize them to what is happening around you; for example, you go to wash your hands and spontaneously, a prayer wells up in your heart...Lord, wash away all my sins.

- You are putting your shoes on in the morning, and from your heart flows this thought: Lord, let me walk in your ways this day.

- You witness a beautiful sunset and, spontaneously, a prayer wells up in your heart...Father, thank you for that gift.

After a time, these memorized prayers will eventually become one continual act of love where fewer and fewer words are needed.

Love is present without words.

Some reflections:

The simplicity of this prayer form can cause us to overlook its profound power and the effect it can have not only on our souls but on our bodies as well.

To have a frequent connection with this God we love provides us with a calm reassurance. We are not alone when challenges and difficulties arise.

Francis uses the lovely analogy of a little child holding tight to his father's hand with one hand while gathering berries from the bushes with the other hand. We never let go of our Father's hand as long as we gently thread these little aspirations all through the day.

This second way of praying is, indeed, powerful and grace-filled. I encourage you to attempt to assimilate both the Direction of Intention and the aspirations into your prayer life. It will not happen in a day or a week, or perhaps even a year, but if you stay with it, you will find your heart transformed!

The warning for this beautiful pearl is that you will at times find yourself almost seeming to stand still, and you may grow discouraged, thinking that this really isn't for you. You may begin to think that you will just never arrive at achieving this way of "praying always."

When that happens, my friend, take out your little guidebook and open it to pearl five.

Here, as you have seen, Francis has a remedy for your discouragement and your desire to leave your spiritual journey to go back to your comfortable life as it was before.

Remember that I am praying for you.

When you are ready, I invite you to pearl six.

♣ *Pearl Six* ♣

Be patient with yourself!

"Be patient with everyone, but above all with yourself."

I chose this quote from Francis because it follows the natural course of the other pearls. If we can be authentically our truest selves (pearl one), if we are learning to bloom where we are planted (pearl two), if we are learning to savor each present moment (pearl three), if we are practicing the Direction of Intention and the aspirations (pearls four and five), and they are becoming steadily a natural part of our day, then we have traveled far on the narrow way that leads to holiness!

All that we have discussed and reflected on sounds so simple and so perfect. We must not lose sight of the fact that we still have to deal with our human nature, and all of us struggle with being less than we would like to be, and of often falling back into old habits or weak tendencies in ourselves, despite our resolve to rid ourselves of these weaknesses and failings.

We all deal with becoming discouraged and impatient at our frequent failings, "beating ourselves up" as we would say today. Francis recognized this human tendency to be impatient with ourselves. So let us go to him and read his advice to his directees about this problem:

This letter, written to Mademoiselle de Soulfour, was dated July 22, 1603. Let us listen to his response to her on patience.

"Mademoiselle,

Know that patience is the one virtue which gives greatest assurance of our reaching perfection, and while we must have patience with others, we must also have it with ourselves. Those who aspire to a pure love of God need to be more patient with themselves than with others.

Our imperfections are going to accompany us to the grave. We can't go anywhere without having our feet on the ground, yet we don't just lie there, sprawled in the dust. On the other hand, we mustn't think we can fly, for we are like little chicks that don't have wings yet. We die little by little, so our imperfections must die with us, a little each day. " (Francis de Sales, Jane de Chantal, Letters of Spiritual Direction, p. 98)

Do you remember Madame Brulart? She is becoming a lovely companion on our mountain walk. We keep meeting her! Well, she is back again, this time seeking advice from Francis about her many imperfections.

Remember that she first met Francis in 1604 during Lent. She seems to have begun a regular correspondence with him in May of 1604. This letter is dated March, 1605.

"Madame,

You complain that there is quite an admixture of faults and imperfections in your life in spite of your great desire to attain perfection and the pure love of God. I answer that...it is not possible to empty ourselves completely of ourselves. So we must be patient and not think that we can overcome in a day, all the bad habits we have acquired through the poor care we have taken of our spiritual health. We must, little by little, and step by step, acquire that self-mastery which the saints took years to acquire. Please be patient with everyone, but above all with yourself." (Francis de Sales, Jane de Chantal, Letters of Direction, p. 108)

Some reflections:

- Patience with ourselves is easier said than done. For some of us, it is a lifelong struggle.

- Patience with ourselves can be the best gift we ever allowed into our heart, but it will only happen if we have a supple, surrendered heart. If we persist in dark judgments on ourselves and others, we block God's desire to heal and forgive.

A caution for pearl six:

This pearl may take longer to absorb than the others. Many persons hold lifelong habits of being disappointed and discouraged with themselves. There is always the temptation to just give up the fight.

Please give your heart the time it needs to surrender to this attitude of gentleness with ourselves. It will be well worth the wait, I promise you!

When we can forgive ourselves and others, peace enters into our soul. We will examine this peace later in pearl eight. Take a little pause on our path and when you feel rested, we will first explore pearl seven.

♣ *Pearl Seven* ♣

Practice the little virtues.

I think you have learned from this journey that Francis has a spirituality that is gentle and simple, accessible to all. In many of his letters of direction, he encourages his directees to love and practice the little virtues of gentleness, humility, kindness toward each neighbor, patience, modesty, temperance…and the list goes on.

In his book, *Introduction to the Devout Life,* Francis reminds us that, "Occasions are not often presented for the exercise of fortitude, magnanimity, and great generosity, but meekness, temperance, modesty, and humility are virtues by which all the actions of our life should be tempered." (Intro III, p.137)

We will continue with the letter he wrote to Mademoiselle de Soulfour while she was still a young religious struggling with the defects she found both in herself and in her fellow religious. Here is what he writes to her about her situation:

"Let us stay at our Lord's feet, like Mary Magdalene and **practice those ordinary virtues suited to our littleness - little peddler, little pack -** *these are the virtues which are better practiced in going downhill than in climbing, and suit our legs better:* **patience, forbearance toward our neighbor, service of others, humility, gentleness of heart, affability, tolerance of our own imperfections, and similar little virtues.** *I do not say that we are not to ascend by prayer, but to do so* **one step at a time."** (Francis de Sales, Jane de Chntal, Letters of Spiritual Direction, p.98)

Francis is so practical! How true it is that we are not often in a circumstance where we must practice heroic virtue, but many times a day we will find occasion to practice the little virtues.

Some reflections:

- I think we might be tempted to believe that the practice of these little virtues requires too much concentration and attention. It could prove to be almost impossible when our minds are busy with handling the responsibilities and challenges of each day.

- Can we really spend time attempting to be gentle when the baby is crying in his crib, the soup on the stove is just about to boil over, the phone is ringing, and three text messages just came on our cell phone?

- If we have worked at nurturing gentleness in our attitudes and thoughts, then the chances are good that we will be a lot better equipped to stay calm when all of the above is happening. This is a good time to attempt reciting a short mantra such as, "Lord, lead me to gentleness."

As we absorb more and more all of the beautiful and practical spirituality contained in the Salesian pearls, an attitude of gentleness will begin to grow within us quite naturally, almost without our realizing it. Remember the parable of Jesus about sowing seed: "But some seed fell on rich soil and produced fruit, a hundred, or sixty, or thirtyfold." (Mt 13: 8)

As you faithfully attempt to live Salesian spirituality, something happens in your heart and you will find yourself, I believe, becoming more gentle, more patient, more loving.

Is there a warning I would give you about this pearl? All of this could perhaps seem like too much, or seem too hard to achieve. Hold firm to your yearning for holiness, and just keep going one step at a time.

When you feel you are ready, we will explore pearl eight.

♣ *Pearl Eight* ♣

Be at peace!

Francis, from his long years of directing souls, knew how important it was to learn to maintain peace within our hearts, a peace despite failings and weaknesses, a peace despite sufferings and challenges in our lives, a peace despite all that might be happening around us and within us.

This peace, if we could maintain it, would be like the mariner's compass...in the midst of darkness and tempestuous storms, the mariner depends on the compass to keep his bearings and to steer a steady course.

Francis wants us to know a deep peace that nothing can shake and, as you can imagine, to have this peace, we would need a deep and unflagging trust in God. It means that our trust would remain steadfast even when our souls and even our hearts might be in deep darkness...unable to sense God's presence, unable to feel it, but to trust that God is there, right in the midst of our darkness.

Our words from Francis for this peace pearl come from the little *Golden Counsels*, a booklet composed of small excerpts of his teachings.

"Do not look forward to the mishaps of this life with anxiety, but await them with a perfect confidence so that when they do occur, God, to whom you belong, will deliver you from them.

He has kept you up to the present; remain firmly in the hands of his providence, and he will help you. When you cannot walk, he will carry you.

Do not think of what will happen tomorrow, for the same eternal Father who takes care of you today will look out for you tomorrow and every day. Either he will keep you from evil or he will give you invincible courage to endure it.

First thing in the morning, prepare your heart

to be at peace; then throughout the day to call it back to that peace frequently, and as it were, to again take your heart in your hands. Be at peace! (Golden Counsels)

Peace be with you...be not afraid!

This was the very first message of the angels to men on Christmas night when our Savior came to live among us; they sang out with all their angelic splendor, "Glory to God in the highest, and on earth peace to those on whom his favor rests." (Lk 2:14)

Peace was proclaimed by Jesus immediately following his resurrection from the dead. The Scriptures tell us that each time he appeared to his apostles, his opening words were: "Peace be with you." (Jn 20:19)

So peace is a precious gift, originating in heaven itself!

Some reflections:

- How can one truly be at peace when everything is topsy-turvy all around us? Is it not almost impossible?

- How can one be at peace when there is violence and abuse and terrorism and fear for the future bombarding us every day?

- Is feeling peaceful a purely emotional action or does it have to include the will?

- Have you known in your life a person who seemed always to be calm and peaceful even in a crisis? How did this impress you?

- Do we desire this peace strongly enough to want take the trouble to make it happen in our lives? What are some things we would need to change in ourselves to acquire this peace?

Lots of food for reflection!

I would simply recommend that you gently bring yourself back to peace when you find yourself becoming agitated and worried. Take as a mantra, when you find your peace weakening, the words of Jesus himself when he appeared to his apostles after his resurrection:

Peace be with you! Be not afraid!

Our first-time journey together is coming soon to an end, but I hope you understand now that this journey will circle back and begin over again many, many times. I hope you will find yourself coming back frequently to this little guidebook. As I wrote in my beginning message, the journey will last a lifetime. We will fall many times, but let us be resolved never to quit the walk.

We have gathered some very beautiful and very profound pearls of wisdom from Francis. This last one is meant to crown all the others:

I invite you to pearl nine, our very last pearl!

♣ *Pearl Nine* ♣

Live + Jesus

This beautiful phrase comes right from the heart of Salesian spirituality. Francis used it frequently in his letters of spiritual direction. The essence of these words, for Francis, meant that we must take on the mind and the heart of Jesus and live each moment and in each event as Jesus lived.

The disciple becomes like the master!

Francis was drawing from St. Paul who tells the world, "I live now, no longer I, but Christ lives in me." (Gal 2:20)

How does this happen? *Live Jesus*?

Francis tells us that it happens when we have totally surrendered ourselves to the Will of God in each present moment.

The best background for this pearl comes from the *Introduction to the Devout Life* published by Francis in 1609. The following excerpt is taken from this book:

"I wish, therefore, dear Philothea, to engrave and inscribe on your heart, before anything else, this holy and sacred maxim: LIVE JESUS! After that, I am sure that your life which comes from your heart, like the almond tree from its kernel, will produce all its actions, which are its fruits, inscribed and engraved with the same word of salvation. Just as this gentle Jesus will live in your heart, he will live also in your conduct and appear in your eyes, in your mouth, in your hands, even in your hair. Then you could say reverently following St. Paul, I live now, not I but Christ lives in me (Galatians 2:20). In short, he who has won the heart of man, has won the whole man." (Wisdom from St. Francis de Sales and St. Jane de Chantal, p. 132)

Francis desires that we take on the mind, the heart, and the attitude of Jesus. Jesus was the divine model for us in accomplishing the will of the Father in all things.

Jesus' words in the Garden of Gethsemane, "Father, not my will, but thine be done," must become our words and our mantra of surrender to all that the Father desires.

Some reflections:

- This surrender will not happen easily, but if we make a habit of it in little things, then when the big crosses come, we will find the strength we need.

- There is an expression that was very popular a few years ago and can still be found today: **WWJD** – what would Jesus do? Sometimes you will see people wearing these letters on bracelets or on t-shirts to remind themselves to live **WWJD.** Well, my friend, pearl nine is Francis' version **of WWJD**!

Some caution:

We have been on a beautiful but sometimes arduous journey. You have discovered and contemplated many of the most common and most beloved components of what is now familiar to you as "Salesian spirituality."

I offer you the advice that Francis offered in the final lines of the *Introduction to the Devout Life:*

"The world will tell you, Philothea, that I have told you to do so much that you will never have time for anything else. But I have not asked you to do it all every day. There will be time for the other things of life." (Intro. V, p. 324)

St. Francis gave his Philothea (all those who were reading his book) some simple resolutions. I offer you a few of my own.

- Renew your yearning for holiness gently each morning as you begin a new day. No matter how many times you have found yourself falling short of your desires, just begin again patiently.

- **Stay on the journey!** Keep your little guidebook nearby; review parts of it from time to time to keep up your courage. Treasure the pearls of wisdom that it contains.

- Live Jesus!

It has been a delight to travel with you. I hope we will do it together many times. Remember: each time you take up this little guidebook, you are among all those who are carried in prayer each day as I have promised.

If ever you want to share where you are in your journey, or have a question or concern, I am as near as: srjohnm@yahoo.com.

May God's blessings be with you

My dear friend,

As we studied the various pearls, you may have picked up that there are two virtues that are key to authentic Salesian spirituality: humility and gentleness.

To aid you in acquiring these two virtues, I thought it might be beneficial to locate for you a litany of humility and a litany of gentleness.

A litany is a series of phrases or words, often used in the context of prayer. If gentleness is a struggle at any particular time, feel free to draw from this simple litany to refresh and renew yourself as you struggle to be more gentle.

Jesus, meek and humble of heart, hear my prayer.

When I am irritated and upset,
Lord, give me your gentleness.

When I am anxious and worried,
Lord, give me your gentleness.

When I have to confront or correct someone,
Lord, give me your gentleness.

When I am being confronted or corrected,
Lord, give me your gentleness.

When my patience is wearing thin,
Lord, give me your gentleness.

When I am interrupted in what I am doing,
Lord, give me your gentleness.

When it is hard to forgive another,
Lord, give me your gentleness.

When it is hard to forgive myself,
Lord, give me your gentleness.

When I am tired and overworked,
Lord, give me your gentleness.

When I have to deal with another person's anger,
Lord, give me your gentleness.

When I just do not feel very gentle,
Lord, give me your gentleness.

Sacred Heart of Jesus, I trust in you.

If you happen to be struggling with being humble, this little prayer might prove helpful. Feel free to recite the whole litany or to recite just those phrases that resonate with where you are in your spiritual journey.

O Jesus! meek and humble of heart, Hear me.

From the desire of being esteemed,
   Deliver me, Jesus. (repeat after each line)

From the desire of being loved,
From the desire of being extolled,
From the desire of being honored,
From the desire of being praised,
From the desire of being preferred to others,
From the desire of being consulted,
From the desire of being approved,
From the fear of being humiliated,
From the fear of being despised,
From the fear of suffering rebukes,
From the fear of being calumniated,

From the fear of being forgotten,
From the fear of being ridiculed,
From the fear of being wronged,
From the fear of being suspected,
That others may be loved more than I,

Jesus, grant me the grace to desire it. (repeat after each line)

That others may be esteemed more than I,
That, in the opinion of the world, others
 may increase and I may decrease,
That others may be chosen and I set aside,
That others may be praised and I unnoticed,
That others may be preferred to me in
everything,
That others may become holier than I, provided
that I may become as holy as I should,

This beautiful litany is attributed to Cardinal
Merry del Val (1865-1930), who was Secretary
of State to Pope Pius X.

Cited Works

Francis de Sales, Jane de Chantal: Letters of Spiritual Direction, translated by Péronne Marie Thibert, V.H.M.; selected and introduced by Wendy M. Wright and Joseph F. Power, O.S.F.S. Copyright © 1988 by Péronne Marie Thibert, V.H.M., Wendy M. Wright, and Joseph F. Power, O.S.F.S. Paulist Press, Inc., Mahwah, NJ. Reprinted by permission of Paulist Press, Inc. www.paulistpress.com

Golden Counsels of St. Francis de Sales. Edited by Mary Paula McCarthy VHM, Mary Grace McCormack, VHM, translated by Peronne Marie Thiebert, VHM, Stella Niagra, NY: DeSales Resources and Ministries, 2006

In the Midst of the World: A Call to Holiness, translated from German. Brooklyn, NY: The Sisters of the Visitation, 1985

Introduction to the Devout Life, translated and edited by Fr. Antony Mookenthottam, MSFS, Fr. Armind Nazareth, MSFS, Fr. Antony Kolencherry, MSFS . Bangalore, INDIA: St. Paul Press, 2005

Live Jesus: Wisdom from Saints Francis de Sales and Jane de Chantal. Louise Perrota, General Editor. Ijamsville, MD: The Word Among Us Press, 2000

Spiritual Directory of St. Francis de Sales: Reflections for the Laity. Commentary by Lewis S. Fiorelli. Boston, MA: Daughters of Saint Paul, 1985

Thy Will Be Done: Letters to Persons in the World. Manchester, NH: Sophia Press, 1995